A Is for Autism, F Is for Friend

A Is for Autism, F Is for Friend

A Kid's Book on Making Friends with a Child Who Has Autism

Joanna L. Keating-Velasco

AAPC

P.O. Box 23173
Shawnee Mission, Kansas 66283-0173
www.asperger.net

© 2007 Autism Asperger Publishing Co.
P.O. Box 23173
Shawnee Mission, Kansas 66283-0173
www.asperger.net

Publisher's Cataloging-in-Publication

Keating-Velasco, Joanna L.

    A is for autism, F is for friend : a kid's book on making
friends with a child who has an autism spectrum disorder /
Joanna L. Keating-Velasco. -- 1st ed. -- Shawnee Mission,
Kan. : Autism Asperger Pub. Co., 2007.

        p. ; cm.
    ISBN-13: 978-1-931282-43-7
    ISBN-10: 1-931282-43-9
    LCCN: 2007922523
    Audience: ages 8-12.
    Includes bibliographical references.

        1. Autism in children--Juvenile literature. 2. Friendship--
Juvenile literature. 3. Social acceptance in children--Juvenile
literature. I. Title.

RJ506.A9 K43 2007
618.92/85882--dc22   0703

Illustrations ©2007 JupiterImages Corporation

This book is designed in American Typewriter and Times New Roman.

Printed in the United States of America.

Special Acknowledgments

Special thanks and love to Kristina Velasco,
my daughter (age 11), for helping me write this at
an upper-elementary level.

Recognition to Temple Grandin for inspiring
me to better understand how the mind of autism
functions.

Admiration to "Chelsea," a fictional character
created from a rainbow of special kids.

Additional thanks to all those aides, teachers,
parents, and especially students,
who taught me so much.

And finally, dedicated to my friend, Jon …
you taught me to look deeper into your eyes
and see the wonder, love and unique qualities
of autism and friendship.

Table of Contents

Greetings
from Chelsea

Hello, my name is Chelsea, and I am 11 years old. I am in the fifth grade. I don't know if you recognize me, but I see you every day at recess. I notice that you have a lot of friends, and it seems like you all have a good time together on the playground. I think I might enjoy some of the games you play. It looks like it might be cool to be one of your friends.

Here is the challenge, though. I have a disorder called autism, which can make it hard for me to make friends. You seem to be good at making friends. How about if I tell you more about me, so we can get to know each other?

What in the World Is Autism?

Autism is called a "spectrum disorder," which means that people with autism have a lot of different symptoms and behaviors; some are more obvious than others.

I like to describe autism using a rainbow. There is a huge rainbow of people, each with a variety of abilities, talents and challenges. Each person with autism (as well as any other person, for that matter) is a completely unique individual; no two are exactly the same.

I have what some people call "severe autism," which means that I am on one end of the rainbow. You would probably notice my symptoms and behaviors pretty quickly (like covering my ears, spinning, flapping my arms or making funny noises).

Other kids on the rainbow of autism have Asperger Syndrome, which is sometimes called high-functioning autism. Kids with Asperger Syndrome are better able to communicate with you through speech. I sometimes prefer using a keyboard or picture cards (I will explain what those are later). Regardless of where a kid falls on that rainbow of autism, making friends and expressing emotions can be tricky.

Autism changes the way the brain usually works. Brains of kids with autism work differently than those without, which can make language (talking) and social interaction (playing) difficult. Brains are kind of like computers. Some process information better and faster than others.

I heard that 1 out of 150 children are born with autism. That's a lot of kids on the autism rainbow. Over one million people in the United States today have some form of autism. Also, autism is four times more likely in boys than in girls! I am in a special day class for students with autism, so I end up being around a bunch of boys most of the day. I don't get a lot of "girl time" in the classroom.

TALK TIME

1. What is one thing about autism that you just learned that you didn't know?

2. Describe a time (if any) when you came into contact with a child who has autism. How did you know he or she had autism? Did someone tell you, or did you notice certain behaviors? Share different behaviors you noticed.

3. If you had autism, do you think you would want to be known as "an autistic kid"? How can we avoid labeling others solely by how they are different?

"Sensing" the Differences

I have told you a little about autism, the disorder, but what about me?

I'm a girl who happens to have autism. In order to help us better understand each other, I'd like to tell you about some of my issues or challenges. Knowing them will help make it easier for us to be friends. First of all, I have a lot of sensory issues.

The five senses are:
1. Sight
2. Hearing
3. Touch
4. Smell
5. Taste

Let me tell you about some sensory issues that are challenging for me.

SIGHT – DO YOU SEE WHAT I SEE?

I have an amazing sense of sight. When I walk into a room, I notice an incredible number of details. However, sometimes taking it all in can be a challenge for me. For example, when I visit our  school's kindergarten class, I am overwhelmed by everything … the posters on the walls, the bubbling fish tank, the streamers hanging from the ceiling holding artwork, the rat running around the cage, the colorful carpet and the bright lights that cause a strange reflection on everything.

At times, it can be a bit too much for my eyes to handle and can make it hard for me to concentrate on my work. I have to admit though, I really enjoy going to the kindergarten room to feed their class rat!

Even though too much visual stuff can be overwhelming to me, I am what is called a visual learner and learn best when things are presented to me in pictures. In my classroom, we have visual schedules and reminders (which I'll talk more about later) that help focus me.

HEARING – TURN THAT DOWN ... IT'S TOO LOUD!

Have you ever been to a concert or an amusement park when all of a sudden it just got too loud and you covered your ears with your hands? Or what about when someone scratches his fingers down a chalkboard? Ouch!

My hearing is sometimes "amplified," meaning I have the volume set too high. Sounds that you may not even notice might be blasting into my ears. For example, when you go to the library, you might find it very quiet. However, I hear all sorts of noises like someone typing away on a computer, someone tapping a pencil on a desk, or the air condition humming – those kinds of things can really bother me.

I usually cover my ears with my hands to make me feel better. I am not trying to be rude. I just want to turn down the volume, or shut off the pain. Sometimes I behave in ways that may seem strange to you. I do that to avoid the possibility of a loud noise shrieking in my ears (like someone acting like they are going to pop a balloon, yikes!). Sudden loud sounds (like a crowd cheering for an awesome soccer goal) can startle me and cause me to panic. I may cover my ears or try to quickly leave the area to escape from the noise.

TOUCH – GETTING IN TOUCH WITH ME

Here's a subject that's touchy with me (tee hee). I have some major issues with "touch," but I really do like to shake hands and hug people. The problem is that if you approach to hug me, I might not be ready for that waterfall of energy that goes through my body when somebody touches me. It's kind of like getting a static shock, ouch!

The sense of touch is confusing to my body. However, if I approach you and start the hug or handshake, my body is ready for what is coming, and everything's fine. Or if you ask me ahead of time if you can shake my hand, I can try to prepare my body for that sense of touch.

It's kind of like when you tickle yourself – it doesn't really tickle because you know it's coming, but if someone else sneaks up on you and tickles you, it can drive you crazy! Sometimes I need more of a warning to accept the sense of touch. My soccer coach always asks me, "Chelsea, can I have a high five?" I love to give him high fives – especially after I score a goal.

SMELL – THE BIONIC NOSE KNOWS

My sense of smell can be so strong that my dad calls me "the bionic nose." This gift can come in handy when I smell something yummy like brownies, but sometimes it can make me feel miserable.

Some smells that you may not even notice can make my stomach feel upset. For example, if my Girl Scout leader is working closely with me on a project, I can get nauseated by the smell of her cucumber melon body spray combined with her Starbucks' coffee breath and the stinky markers in her hand.

You might not even notice these scents, but the combination of them makes me want to gag. Then again, maybe you've experienced this, too. Have you ever been visiting a pet store when the cages were dirty and smelly? I'll bet you couldn't wait to get away from that smell. Occasionally, I feel the same way, so I just have to leave that area and go somewhere else.

TASTE ... YOU THINK YOU'RE A PICKY EATER?

Maybe we are the same in this area. Some kinds of food just give me the "heebie jeebies." Just looking at a strawberry totally grosses me out. And if someone "infects" my plate of food by putting a strawberry on it, I get really upset.

Sometimes I don't like a food because of its color, texture or shape. Did you ever eat something really slimy and simply didn't like it because of the texture?

Of course, there are a lot of foods that I really like. My favorites are spaghetti and pizza. How about you? What are your favorite foods?

JUST A BIT OF COMMON "SENSE"

I hope I have given you an idea of some of my "sensory" issues. You might experience some of these issues yourself. Is there a food that you think is slimy and yucky? Do you ever get really frustrated when sounds around you are too loud, or your brother or sister won't stop making annoying noises? Has anyone ever snuck up and grabbed you from behind to surprise you … only to make you feel frightened?

We probably share some of these sensory issues, right?

TALK TIME

1. Look around the room you are in right now. Now think about your senses. Do you see, hear or smell anything that might be distractive or annoying for someone with autism based on what I just told you? Give one example and explain how that item makes you feel and how you think it might make someone with autism feel. Is there something in this room that distracts you?

2. Is there a food item that you think is totally disgusting? Why? If someone put it on your dinner plate, how would you feel, or what would you do? Could you just ignore it? Would you eat it?

3. Have you ever been trying to do your homework and it was too noisy or distracting in the room? What were some of the things that distracted you? How did you handle the distractions? Were you able to ignore them or did you have to move away or ask somebody to do something different?

Can You See What I Am Thinking?

S omething about me that I find really cool is that I am a "visual thinker." I think in pictures; you probably think more "verbally" (with words). When someone mentions something to me, I go back into my memory bank (mental photo album) and find a picture from my past that I think represents whatever the person is talking about. Of course, this happens really fast, so I hardly notice it.

Let me explain. Let's say we are both making macaroni and cheese – something I love, by the way. You may read the box and follow the written directions. I, on the other hand, will play a video in my head showing the visual steps of how the macaroni and cheese is prepared. Either way, we both achieve the same outcome (yummy dinner!), but we take different paths to arrive there.

Because I think using pictures, it helps me to be shown "visuals" in addition to talking to me; this is especially true if I have to follow directions. There are a lot of different visual helpers I use. My favorite is my own customized book full of little picture cards that I can pull out to show people what I want or need, or how I feel. My favorite card shows a photo of French fries.

Also, my teacher uses visual schedules and picture reminders in our classroom to help us stay on task or switch from one activity to another. For example, my teacher might ask me to be quiet, and I may not understand her (ever happen to you, ha!).

Sometimes my ears don't connect to my brain (like when your mom asks you ten times to clean your room while you are watching cartoons and you don't hear her at all). To help me better understand when I hear "be quiet," my teacher might show me a picture of a face with a quiet mouth. Because that is visual – remember I am a visual thinker – it becomes clear to me right way.

Actually, everybody uses visual helpers. They may just not think about it that way. Your homework binder reminds you about your class assignments and tests. Those Scout Laws you have posted in your meeting room remind you how to behave with honor. On your cell phone, that flashing icon of an envelope shows you someone left you a voicemail message. And, of course, the clock on your kitchen wall tells you when it's dinner time!

IDIOMS ... SAY WHAT YOU MEAN, PLEASE!

Because I think visually, it's confusing when people use idioms (terms or expressions that don't make sense if taken literally) when talking with me. One day I was getting really stressed out in class and my teacher said, "Chelsea, get a hold of yourself," so I grabbed my arms and squeezed tight. She giggled and said, "No, I meant relax and go take a break." I still don't know why "get a hold of yourself" means the same thing as "relax."

There are a lot of what teachers call "idioms" or "figures of speech" that I just don't get. Think of the sayings below in pictures and you'll understand what I mean.

- Take a seat (where do you want me to take it?)
- Get over it! (get over what?)
- She got up on the wrong side of the bed (which side should you get up on?)
- Backseat driver (my dad calls my mom this all the time, but she's in the *front* seat!)
- Don't spill the beans (what beans? where are the beans?)

Talk Time

1. Close your eyes. Think of the word "car" in your mind. Did you get a picture of some sort of a car (like your mom's or perhaps your favorite model?), or did your mind start flipping through pages and pages of cars that you have seen in the past? Compare different images you saw with what others around you saw. Did any of you have the same image?

2. Can you think of an idiom or figure of speech that you use that, taken literally (word for word), would be confusing for someone with autism based on what we just talked about? How could you better phrase that so that someone with autism could easily understand what you meant?

Look Deep into My Eyes

Does your mom ever say this to you? "Look at me when I am talking to you!" I get this statement a lot. I have trouble keeping eye contact. If you want me to look into your eyes, I may have trouble listening. It's hard for me to do both at the same time.

Also, I usually feel really weird or scared when people look into my eyes while they are talking to me. So, I look away, because it makes me feel safer.

Another issue regarding eye contact is that it is difficult for me to read the "message" that you are sending with your eyes. It is hard for me to know just by looking at a person's eyes or face if he is happy, sad, angry or just completely bored with what's happening. I don't always understand that connection.

You might not even notice how important eye contact is in your daily life. I'm sure there are times when you have walked up to a friend, looked into his eyes and asked him, "what's wrong?" You simply understood that his eyes were saying he was sad without him saying a word.

I find it interesting how much information *you* are able to see about how someone is feeling simply by looking at his eyes. You might be mad about something and show it with your eyes, but for me, it's easier if you just tell me or show me a picture of how you feel.

Talk Time

1. Have you ever even thought about eye contact before?

2. Do you ever have difficulty having eye contact with anyone? If so, why? How does that make you feel?

3. If you were telling a friend something important and she was not looking in your direction while you were talking, how would you feel?

4. Try this. Get a partner and have a 30-second conversation while maintaining eye contact the entire time. Did you enjoy the constant eye contact or was it awkward?

5. With that same partner, have one of you choose an emotion (sad, happy, mad, confused or surprised) without telling the other what you chose. Using your eyes and facial expression only, show that emotion. Could your partner guess your emotion? Switch roles and try again.

6. Can you think of situations where not being able to read a person's emotions using facial expressions or eyes would make life more challenging?

Echo, Echo!

Another difficulty I face is echolalia (**ech·o·la·li·a**). You might ask, "Echo what what?" Well, that's actually similar to what echolalia really is.

Echolalia is basically me repeating what you just said or echoing you. You'll hear me do this a lot. For example, if you are asking me, "How are you today?" instead of me saying, "Fine," I repeat back, "How are you today?"

I know it can get frustrating for you if I mimic you, but you can sometimes help by giving me answers or some words to help me along the way. I am trying to communicate, but I am kind of skipping a little like a scratched CD. So, if I just repeat you when you ask me a question, you can help me answer.

There is a special kind of echolalia, called *delayed echolalia*. That is when I repeat phrases that I have heard a while back. Occasionally, you may also hear me repeat portions of scripts from a favorite movie or television show. When something is bothering me, I sometimes do this to feel more comfortable. My mom calls this "video talk." I am able to recite complete scenes from some of my Disney videos. Some people find this very interesting.

Talk Time

1. Let's try "echolalia." Pick a partner. One person talks first and the other person repeats every word or phrase the first person says. Try out a conversation like that for 30 seconds. How did it feel being the first person whose words kept getting repeated?

2. Why do you think someone with autism might repeat everything you say?

3. How could you help a person deal with echolalia?

What Are You Doing?

At the park, you may have seen me rock back and forth, spin or flap my hands. People have told me it looks strange when I do this, but it makes me feel better. Sometimes my body just feels "out of sync," and that is when these kinds of behaviors give me comfort. Basically, they help me control a confusing signal coming from my brain. It's like the feeling you get when you are dizzy and you have to sit down to center yourself.

If I am doing one of these behaviors and you want me to stop, I can usually stop if you let me know. Sometimes I don't even realize I am doing this until someone tells me.

I bet you do things at times that look strange to other people, too. Can you think of any? My parents sometimes dance around the house. I think they look weird when they do this, but they're having fun!

Talk Time

1. Has a brother, sister or friend ever told you that you were acting strange or weird? What were you doing when they said that? Were you able to stop the behavior? Were you enjoying the activity before they tried to stop you?

2. Do you have a brother, sister or friend who sometimes makes loud or annoying noises? How does that make you feel? How do you handle these situations?

From Frustrations to Friendships

You probably get frustrated at times. For example, have you ever been trying to do your math homework and then don't remember or understand what your teacher explained earlier in the day? Then you ask your mom to help, and she has no clue how to add fractions! Argh!

I get frustrated a lot, too. When I want to tell someone how I feel, I have trouble expressing my feelings. Occasionally, I try to ask for something, but I can't get the words out. I can see a picture in my head of exactly what I want, but the words just aren't there. It's like when your computer freezes up or doesn't respond quickly enough. Sometimes I don't feel well, and I don't know what to say.

Since I have trouble communicating these things, I get very frustrated. I might act out by having a tantrum or "a meltdown," as my dad calls it.

I might get really angry and flop down onto the ground, kicking and screaming. If I do this while you are around, you can just take a break from me or get an adult to help.

It can be very frustrating having all of these thoughts, feelings, wants and ideas floating around in my head in pictures and not being able to share them with others.

Well, enough of what annoys me. There are so many things that don't bother me.

Here are some activities I love to do:

- Play video games
- Watch DVDs
- Listen to music on my iPod
- Watch TV
- Swim
- Ride bikes
- Run
- Surf the Internet
- Build sandcastles at the beach
- Jump on a trampoline
- Play in the snow
- Draw pictures and paint

Do you like to do any of these activities? What else do you like to do?

One of my favorite hobbies is an art class I take at the community center. I am very good at painting. If you give me a photograph of a flower, I can paint a picture that looks just like it. One time I won first prize at an art contest for one of my paintings, and my mom framed it and hung it in our living room. She smiled and called it a "Monet." I asked her what that means, and she explained that Monet was a famous painter who lived in France.

At home, I enjoy working with modeling clay. I can take a plain piece of clay and sculpt it into some amazing animals. My specialty is creating elephants.

Sometimes I have a hard time finding something interesting and fun to do. I've seen you playing tetherball at the community center, and it looks like fun. I might like to try to play that game. Maybe you could teach me? I am very good at learning rules. You could also show me where to stand in line and tell me when it's my turn. It's easier if you are direct with me and don't use too many words. For example, if you want me to stand in line, tell me, "Please, stand here," and point to the ground where you want me to stand. Sometimes it's hard for me to understand too many words at once. It helps if you keep it simple and give me time to think about what you say.

Talk Time

1. Next time you meet someone with autism, what can you do to make him or her feel more comfortable?

2. What activities could you try to do together? What might the person be able to teach you?

3. Do any of your friends have sisters or brothers who have autism? Do you think your friend might want to talk about this issue? How can you support your friend?

4. If you were talking with someone with autism, do you think it would be helpful to use a lot of descriptive words to get your point across? Do you think continuing to repeat your question or words over and over would be helpful? Or do you think giving short, direct statements would be more helpful?

Want to Give It a Try?

I would like to be your friend. Friendship consists of loyalty, honesty and forgiveness. These are qualities I have and that I enjoy in a friend. We all need friends. Imagine what life would be like if we didn't have friends to share our laughter, tears, hopes and dreams. Together, we can learn a lot from each other while we have fun.

Sometimes you may not like it if I act annoying, loud, weird or unfriendly. But now I think you have a better understanding of why this happens and that it isn't anything I do deliberately to be strange or rude. Perhaps if you see me at the mall, at McDonald's or on the playground, you could stop by and say, "Hello" to me.

Let's get to know each other. Some people have told me that people with autism are like a puzzle piece trying to fit in. I'm not sure about that, but if that's the case, I hope you will help me complete the puzzle by being my friend.

Want to Know More?

For more information about autism and autism awareness, take a look at the following. The materials can often be checked out of your school or community library. If they don't have these materials, maybe they can order them.

WEBSITES

The following websites have lots of good information about autism and people with autism written specifically for children and young people.

www.angelfire.com/pa5/as/talkingtokids.html

www.asperger.net/index_childrens_stories.htm

www.cdc.gov/ncbddd/kids/kautismpage.htm

www.cyh.com (search autism)

www.delautism.org/kids_only.htm

www.kidshealth.org/kid (search autism)

http://library.thinkquest.org/5852/autism.htm

www.unlockingautism.org/kidscorner.asp

BOOKS

All About My Brother by Sarah Peralta
This illustrated book helps typically developing
children understand that a child with autism is a
child first, and is someone interesting to know.
Sarah gives insight into the sibling relationship in
a way only a child would know. The book is heart-
warming and introspective, with a writing style that
makes it appropriate for children and adults alike.
ISBN: 1-931282-11-0

Ann Drew Jackson by Joan Clark
Friendships expose people to new worlds and
experiences. For Jackson, a project at a new
elementary school is just the passport he needs to
explore a real friendship. *Ann Drew Jackson* is a
story about a surprising friendship that blossoms
between a boy with Asperger Syndrome and a girl
who is dealing with issues of her own. Through
their relationship events occur that teach them to
appreciate each other for the unique individuals
they are. *Ann Drew Jackson* is the sequel to
Jackson Whole Wyoming, also by Joan Clark.
ISBN: 1-931282-45-5

Autism Through a Sister's Eyes by Eve B. Band &
Emily Hecht
Told in her own voice, 10-year-old Emily explains
her feelings and her search for answers about why
her brother Daniel did the things he did. Not only
uplifting, *Autism Through A Sister's Eyes* offers
valuable information and illustrations which make
it an exceptional book for both brothers and sisters
of autistic siblings. ISBN: 1-885477-71-6

Different Like Me: My Book of Autism Heroes by
Jennifer Elder
This book introduces children age 8 to 12 to
inspirational famous and historical figures from the
worlds of science, art, math, literature, philosophy
and comedy, from Albert Einstein, to Dian Fossey
and Wasily. All excel in their own fields, but are
united by the fact that they often found it difficult
to fit in. This book celebrates individuality. It is a
valuable resource for children, particularly children
with autism, their parents, teachers, caregivers and
siblings. ISBN: 1-843108-15-1

Do You Understand Me? by Sofie Koborg Brøsen
Sofie Koborg Brøsen is 11 years old and, like other children of her age, goes to a mainstream school, loves reading comics and being with her family and her cat, Teddy. But Sofie is not the same as everyone else – she has an autism spectrum disorder. Fed up with being misunderstood by her classmates, she has written a book about her world so others can learn to understand her, and vice versa. Teachers, parents, carers, support workers, children with autism spectrum disorders and their classmates will find this an entertaining, informative and attitude-changing read. ISBN: 1-84310-464-4

I Am Utterly Unique: Celebrating the Strengths of Children with Asperger Syndrome and High-Functioning Autism by Elaine Marie Larson
This book, laid out in an A-to-Z format, celebrates the extraordinary gifts and unique perspectives that children with ASD possess. Each page of this playful alphabet book presents one of these children's many talents and abilities. The kid-friendly illustrations and clever text create a positive portrayal of children with ASD. Designed to help children with ASD grow in self-awareness of their many capabilities, the book also encourages dialogue with siblings, friends, parents and teachers. ISBN: 1-931282-89-7

Ian's Walk: A Story About Autism by Laurie Lears
As Tara and Julie take Ian along on their walk to the park, Julie describes how Ian acts differently from most people. For example, he shows no interest in the food or customers in Nan's Diner and pays attention only to the rotating ceiling fan. Admirably patient with Ian, Julie nevertheless grows angry with his seemingly stubborn ways. Yet her close observations of her brother serve her well when Ian wanders away. By thinking of what Ian likes to do, Julie finds her brother and ushers him home again. Through its simple plot, the story conveys a complex family relationship and demonstrates the ambivalent emotions Julie feels about her autistic brother. Sensitizing readers to these dynamics as well as to the autistic condition, this book offers a valuable, warmly told lesson. ISBN: 0-807534-8-03

My Best Friend Will by Jamie Lowell and Tara Tuchel
This book chronicles the relationship between 11-year-old neurotypical Jamie and her friend Willie, who has autism. Enter Willie's world through Jamie's eyes as it unfolds at school, at home, and at play. In the process, you will gain a rich understanding and appreciation of Willie's many unique qualities and come to accept that these are all a part of who he is. ISBN: 1-931282-75-7

Jackson Whole Wyoming by Joan Clark

His classmates have identified him as a "friend" of Jackson, who has Asperger Syndrome, and now Tyler is tormented by what that means in terms of his own personality. Over the course of this highly readable and swift-moving middle-grade novel (2nd to 6th grade), Tyler resolves this issue and in the process recalls incidents from previous school years, growing in his understanding of this unusual classmate. Written by a speech-language pathologist who works with children with autism spectrum disorders, this novel belongs on the library shelf of any middle-grade classroom. ISBN: 1-931282-72-2

Jay Grows an Alien by Caroline Levine

Jay often feels out of place in the world around him, but doesn't know why. Being called names like "space cadet" and "asp-booger" confuses him even further. He has looked up "asp" in the dictionary and knows he is not an asp, a "small poisonous snake from Egypt." But what is he then? This short novel follows Jay, a young boy with Asperger Syndrome, at school and home. Over the course of the novel, as he deals with bullies, faces the difficulties of a sibling relationship, and befriends a cyborg from outer space, Jay begins to find his place and comes to understand that differences in him and others are unique and special. ISBN: 1-931282-29-3

Running on Dreams by Herb Heiman
Join Brad and Justin as they embark upon several teen benchmarks: the first date, rejection by peers, family pressure to succeed, fitting in with the "right" crowd, experiencing teenage sexuality, and dealing with the "outsider kid" who is perceived as "not cool." This book captures many bittersweet and humorous events that bring new insight to a familiar world – the world of heartbreak for two boys whose relationship starts out quite turbulent but evolves into a friendship of loyalty and trust. ISBN: 1-931282-28-5

Sundays with Matthew by Matthew Lancelle and Jeanette Lesada
This unique and engagingly illustrated children's book is based on the author's experience working with a fifth grader with autism, helping him recognize his own and others' emotions and, in general, interact with people. Since many children and youth with autism have well-defined special interests, it is valuable to determine what those interests are and find ways to use them to reinforce appropriate behavior. This book demonstrates that using a special interest and talent is a proven way to help a child reach his full potential. ISBN: 1-931282-84-6

Ten Things Every Child with Autism Wishes You Knew by Ellen Notbohm
Framed with both humor and compassion, this book defines the top 10 characteristics that illuminate the minds and hearts of children with autism. Ellen's personal experiences as a parent, an autism columnist, and a contributor to numerous parenting magazines come together to create a guide for all who come in contact with a child on the autism spectrum. ISBN: 1-932565-30-2

This Is Asperger Syndrome by Elisa Gagnon and Brenda Smith Myles
Through whimsical black-and-white cartoon drawings, *This Is Asperger Syndrome* introduces siblings, peers and other children to the everyday challenges faced by children with Asperger Syndrome at home or at school. ISBN: 0-9672514-1-9

DVD

Autism and Me by Rory Hoy

Only people with autism truly know what it's like to be autistic – and even then, every autistic individual is unique. In this award-winning DVD, Rory explains in easy-to-understand terms what having autism means for everyday functioning. For example, what it is like not to have a natural inclination to respond when somebody calls you by your name; what it's like to take somebody literally when she has actually used a figure of speech; and what it's like to become confused and overwhelmed by loud noises, crowded spaces, etc.

ISBN: 978-1843-105466

Glossary

ASPERGER SYNDROME (abbreviated to AS) –
used to describe a type of mild or high-
functioning autism. People with AS can be
very smart. They might find challenges in the
following areas: socializing with others, dealing
with emotions, playing and communicating with
others and coping with sensory issues. They can
be very interested in and knowledgeable about a
favorite subject matter.

AUTISM – a disorder that affects how the brain
works and causes people to experience the world
differently from the way most others do. People
with autism can have a hard time communicating
with others and expressing/understanding
emotions. Autism affects a wide variety of
people, each with his/her own unique abilities,
gifts and challenges.

AUTISM SPECTRUM – describes the range
(rainbow) of autism disorders from severe
(many noticeable behaviors and symptoms
such as hand flapping, rocking and lack of
eye contact) to Asperger Syndrome (high-
functioning people who are especially
challenged during social and emotional

situations). The thinking and learning abilities of people on the spectrum can range from severely challenged to gifted.

BEHAVIORS – the way a person reacts to something. For example, when your little brother goes into your room without permission, your "behavior" may be to lock your door and hang up a "keep out" sign.

ECHOLALIA – when somebody repeats back words or phrases spoken to her instead of responding to or answering the person speaking to her. Delayed (happening later) echolalia is defined as echoing a phrase after hearing it earlier. The child might verbally repeat scenes from a favorite video.

IDIOM – figure of speech that means something in your culture, but taken literally (word for word) doesn't make much sense. For example, "ants in your pants" means you can't sit still, not that you actually have ants running around in your jeans.

NEUROLOGICAL – science of the nervous system and its disorders.

SENSORY ISSUES – when a person has challenges related to his/her senses (sight, hearing, taste, touch and smell). For example, too many visual distractions in a room (such as flickering lights, posters, artwork) can make a child with autism feel overwhelmed. Also, certain smells or combinations of smells might cause a child to become nauseated. Sensory issues might also include feeling "underwhelmed" or not reacting to something. For example, a child might not react to the noise of a pot crashing down onto the kitchen floor.

SEVERE AUTISM – type of autism with very noticeable symptoms and behaviors (such as lack of eye contact, spinning, rocking or lining up toys). People with severe autism often have challenges learning to talk as well as learning social skills, like playing with others. Many people with severe autism also have mental retardation and are unable to communicate using spoken words. Instead they may use keyboards, visual picture cards or written words. They may experience many sensory issues (see above).

SYMPTOM – behavior or reaction in a person showing the presence of a disease or disorder. Lack of eye contact is a common "symptom" of autism.

VISUALS – picture-oriented tools that help support kids with autism. Visuals come in many forms, including pictures, physical objects or words *shown to* students to help support their learning. For example, a picture card of a lunch bag could be used to show a student it's time for lunch. Also, a written countdown of numbers (5, 4, 3, 2, 1) could show a student he has 5 more math problems, then 4 more problems, and so on, so that he can see an end to the assignment. We all use visuals, such as calendars, to-do lists, etc.